Copyright illustration
by LaDonna Fabre

This book belongs to

_____.

Let's Go Fishin'!
Charlie's Big Catch

Written by Glenn Lansdale
Illustrated by Haytham Karim
Edited by Heidi Cook
Editing by Robin Hollis (Thanks Mom!)

Charlie stares out the window of his dad's big, red truck into the pouring rain.
Dad is taking him to the cabin for a Special Weekend Trip,
but the weather dampens his spirits.

"Hey Buddy. Do ya know what ya wanna do tomorrow?"
Sadly, Charlie responds, "I want to catch a fish,
but I can't because it's raining."
Dad smiled. "Maybe tomorrow will be better. Let's wait and see!"

"Breakfast's ready!"
Charlie strolls into the kitchen and slumps into the chair.
Dad asks again, "So, what do ya wanna do today?!"
Sighing, Charlie says, "Just watch cartoons, I guess."
Turning to hide a huge smile, Dad says, "OK ... but it's a Beautiful Day outside!"

Charlie runs to the window and yells, "**Let's Go Fishin'**!" Dad says, "Sounds like a Plan! We gotta get our boots, 'cause ya know it's muddy out there!"

Boots on and buckets in hand, Charlie and Dad head outside.
"Let's go look under the rabbit pens for bait." Dad says.
"Earthworms come right to the top of the dirt after rain like that."

Dad and Charlie sit in the truck, ready to head to the pond.
Dad asks, "Did we get everything? Did we get the fishing poles?"
"Check," says Charlie.
"Did we get the tackle boxes?"
"Check."
"Bait?"
"Check."
"How about the snacks for us?"
"Check! I made double sure of that," Charlie exclaimed.
"Then Let's GO!"

Dad and Charlie arrive at the pond's shore and set up their gear.

"Look at the bubbles and waves! They are in there, Dad!" Charlie shouts.

Dad gently whispers, "Yes, they are. We don't want to scare them away, so let's keep our voices low."

"OK, Dad!" Charlie is a little quieter.

They bait their hooks and move apart to cast.
Almost immediately, Charlie yells, "**I think I got one!**"
Before Dad gets over to him, Charlie reels the line in fast.

A big stick flops onto the shore. Charlie's face droops.
Dad laughed quietly. "Maybe next time. Keep trying, Buddy."

They set another worm on the hook, and Charlie casts again.
Dad moves back to his place. They watch the bobbers intently.

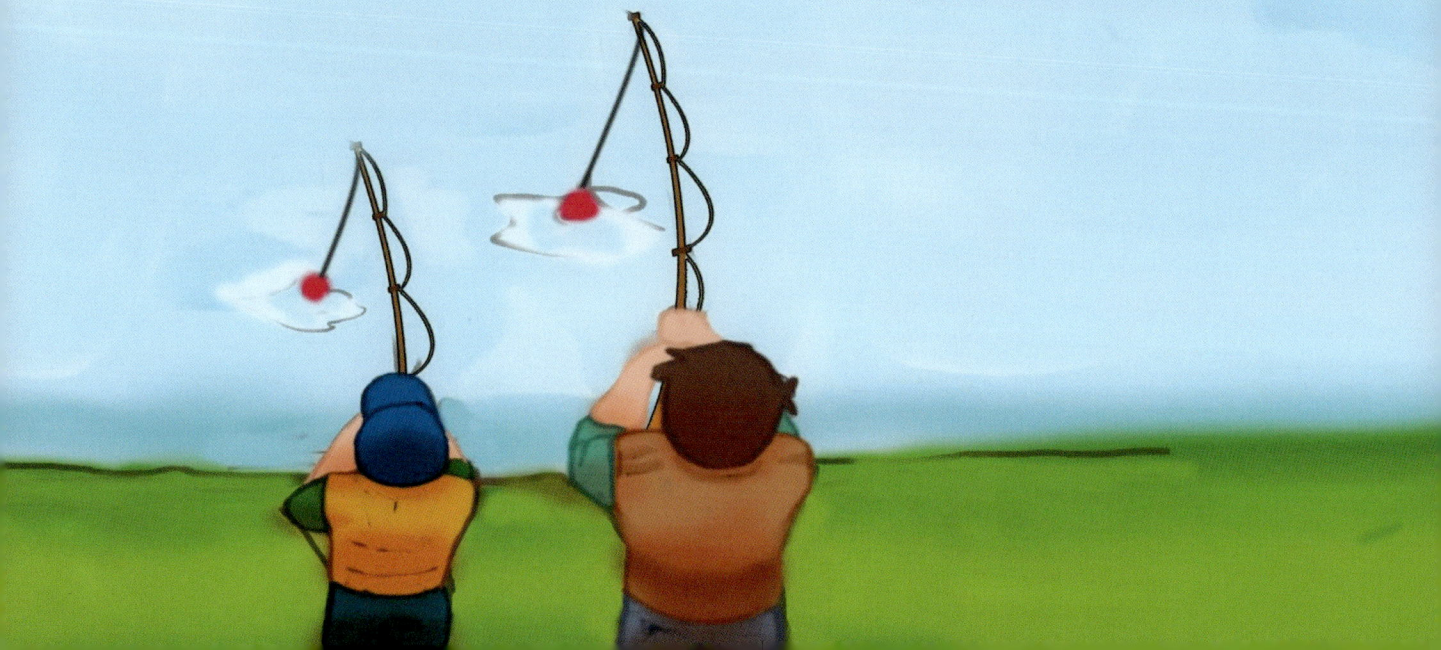

Under the water, the fish swim closer to the bait.
Just as one fish lunges for Charlie's worm, he yells over to Dad.
"Hey Dad! That was a pretty big stick, huh?!" The fish swims away.
Dad chuckles and says softly, "Yeah, it was."

Two fish swim to Charlie's bait. Suddenly, Charlie laughs loudly. The fish dart away.

"What's so funny?" Dad asks.
"I just remembered a joke I heard in school."
"Let's hear it," Dad says.
"What did one fish say to the other fish?"
"What's that?"
Charlie laughs again. **"Keep your mouth shut, and you won't get caught!"**
Dad laughs quietly.

As they finish some snacks, Charlie droops a little.
"We have to go soon, but I haven't caught anything."
Dad rests his hand on Charlie's shoulder.
"One more cast," he says.

Ploop

With the last worm secured on the hook, Charlie casts his best ever.

Ploop! The bobber makes its sound.

Charlie feels something on the line.
Quickly he reels it in, his excitement growing with every turn.

"Ahh, man. Another stick," Charlie says.

Charlie sadly helps to load the truck.
"I bet we'll get 'em next time," Dad says as he starts up the engine.
Charlie does his best to be cheerful.

On the drive back to the cabin, Dad notices the ditch on the side of the road is full of water, so he slows down a little. He sees a splash in the ditch, so he stops the truck.

Charlie asks, "What are you looking at?"

"Let's just see somethin'," Dad says.

They get out of the truck and look in the ditch. **"There's a Huge Fish in there!"** Charlie yells. Dad explains, "The rain last night must've caused the pond to flood, and this fish got carried away to the ditch."

Charlie jumps up and down. "Can we catch it?!"
"I bet you can, Charlie!"
"But how?" Charlie remembers, "We used all our worms."

Dad takes a piece of sandwich out of his bag, puts it on Charlie's hook, and says, "Let's try that."

Charlie slowly lowers his line into the water.

Less than a minute later, he whoops and hollers. **"I Got It!"** The reel feels different this time with a live fish instead of a stick!

Dad quickly grabs a bucket from the back
of the truck, puts a little water in it, and helps his son
put the fish in the bucket.
"**You did it!**" Dad says proudly.
"Now what?" Charlie asks.
Dad says, "I have an idea."

Charlie and Dad--both holding the bucket--take the fish back to the pond where it belongs.

"Now it'll be there for us to catch the next time we come," Dad says.

Thank You

To God for His Grace
To my friends and family for their support
To my Dad for always taking me fishing
To my Pap-pa Charlie for inspiring the name of my character

And... Thank You to the best place a boy could grow up; Warren, Arkansas, in Bradley County; a place whose natural beauty and charm makes adventures like this possible every day.

About the Author

Glenn Lansdale is an author and outdoor enthusiast who has spent his career organizing and promoting special events for adults and children of all ages, including those with special needs.

Glenn wants to stress the importance of spending time with loved ones and enjoying nature. He encourages everyone to look for the opportunities that come from all obstacles.